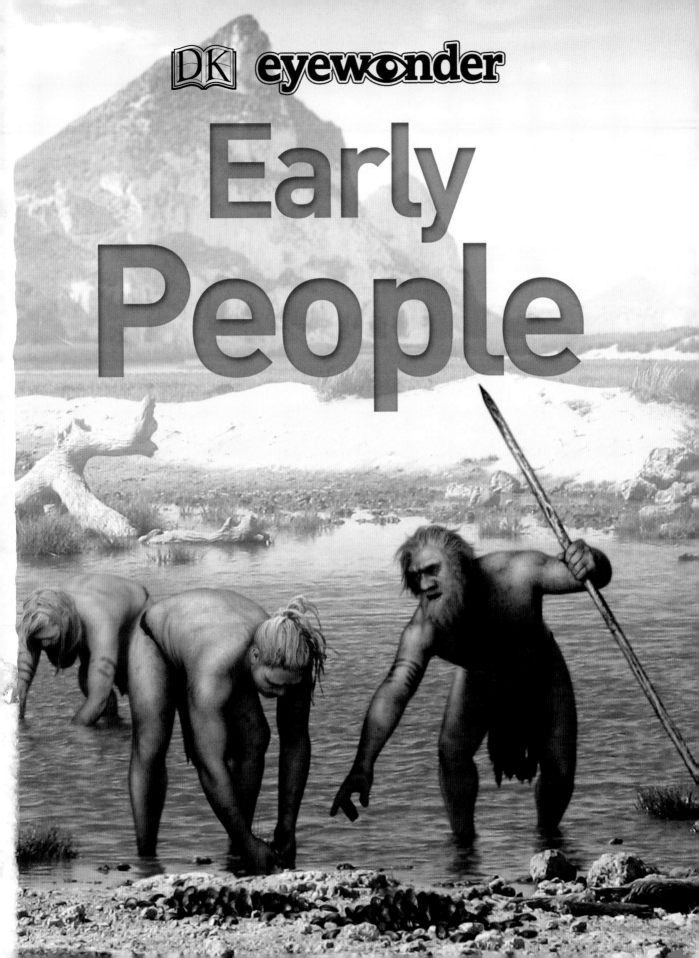

DK eyewonder

Early People

LONDON, NEW YORK,
MELBOURNE, MUNICH, and DELHI

DK UK
Written by Jim Pipe
Senior editor Caroline Stamps
Senior art editor Rachael Grady
Managing editor Gareth Jones
Managing art editor Philip Letsu
Jacket editor Maud Whatley
Jacket designer Mark Cavanagh
Jacket design development manager Sophia MTT
Producer (print production) Mary Slater
Producer (pre-production) Adam Stoneham
Publisher Andrew Macintyre
Consultant John Haywood

DK INDIA
Project editor Bharti Bedi
Project art editor Nishesh Batnagar
Editor Ishani Nandi
Art editor Isha Nagar
Assistant art editor Shreya Sadhan
Managing editor Alka Thakur Hazarika
Managing art editor Romi Chakraborty
Managing jacket editor Saloni Singh
Jacket designer Suhita Dharamjit
Senior DTP designer Harish Aggarwal
DTP designers Rajesh Singh Adhikari,
Nityanand Kumar, Dheeraj Singh
Pre-production manager Balwant Singh
Production manager Pankaj Sharma
Picture researcher Aditya Katyal

First published in Great Britain in 2015 by
Dorling Kindersley Limited
80 Strand, London WC2R 0RL

Copyright © 2015 Dorling Kindersley Limited
A Penguin Random House Company

13 14 15 16 17 10 9 8 7 6 5 4 3 2 1
001 – 259179 – 02/15

A CIP catalogue record for this book
is available from the British Library.

ISBN 978-0-2410-1025-9

Printed and bound in China by Hung Hing

Discover more at
www.dk.com

Contents

4-5
First steps

6-7
The clever ape

8-9
Neanderthals

10-11
Modern humans

12-13
The Stone Age

14-15
Living off the land

16-17
The use of fire

18-19
Life in the freezer

20-21
Land of the giants

22-23
The first artists

24-25
Looking good

26-27
The first religions

28-29
Living with animals

30-31
Taming the land

32-33
The age of metal

34-35
Weapons of war

36-37
Ancient China

38-39
Early Australia

40-41
The Americas

42-43
The first towns

44-45
How do we know?

46-47
True or false?

48-49
Head for home

50-51
What's this?

52-53
Which way?

54-55
Glossary

56
Index and
acknowledgements

First steps

About 7 million years ago (mya), a group of apes began to walk on two legs: these were the hominins (a group that includes modern humans and our ancestors). By 4 mya, creatures looking more like us appeared. The best-known of these, *Australopithecus*, existed about 3 mya.

Out of Africa

The earliest human remains have all been found in the eastern and southern parts of Africa, particularly in the Olduvai Gorge in Tanzania. In fact, the name *Australopithecus* means "southern ape".

Ethiopia

Tanzania

South Africa

Ethiopia, Tanzania, and South Africa are important sites for archaeologists.

Walking tall

Walking on two feet makes us good walkers and runners. Standing up also helps us to look out for danger and keep cool, as more of our body is shaded from the Sun. We know that *Australopithecus* walked upright.

These footprints were made in Tanzania 3.5 mya by three Australopithecus *as they walked upright – like us – across volcanic ash.*

A cracking find!

The skull of a 1.75-million-year-old hominin showed that different hominin species lived at the same time. It probably ate fruit, although its huge teeth and powerful jaws earned it the name "Nutcracker Man".

"Nutcracker Man" skull, found in Tanzania

The brown bones show which parts of the skeleton were found.

A famous ancestor

The world's most famous human ancestor is probably a 3.5-million-year-old *Australopithecus* nicknamed "Lucy". At the time of its discovery in Ethiopia in 1974, it was the most complete *Australopithecus* skeleton ever found.

What does it tell us?

A skeleton "talks". For example, the plants early humans ate contained chemicals from the soil they grew in. By studying *Australopithecus* teeth, we know that males tended to stay put, while females joined other family groups once they grew up.

How tall?

Lucy had a mix of ape and human features – she had long dangling arms, but leg bones suited to walking upright. She would have been just over 1 m (3.3 ft) tall.

Reconstructing Lucy

The clever ape

A new human group, *Homo*, appeared 2.4 million years ago, around the time that the Earth's climate began to change. Although they looked like earlier humans, the *Homo* had nimbler hands, smaller teeth, and a much bigger brain.

All brain and no fur

A big brain is pretty useful but can overheat easily. Around 1 mya humans lost most of their body hair. This may have helped them to keep a cool head!

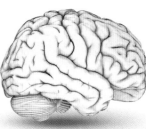

Brain of a modern human

What were the first tools?

Like chimpanzees today, the earliest humans may have used sticks or bones to dig, or defend themselves. The first stone tools appeared about 2.6 mya, but became common after the appearance of *Homo habilis* about 2.4 mya.

Food for thought

Over the last 3 million years, the human brain has grown steadily, tripling in size. This may have been caused by people eating more meat, which provided a rich source of protein.

Homo habilis used simple stone tools to

Homo habilis (2.4–1.6 mya) was the first Homo species and the first to make common use of tools.

Homo ergaster (1.9–1.5 mya) was similar in height and build to a modern human.

Homo erectus (1.8 mya–30,000 years ago) was the first human species to spread outside Africa.

Homo heidelbergensis (600,000–200,000 years ago) evolved into Neanderthals and modern humans.

All in the family

Humans slowly changed, or evolved, over millions of years. By piecing together fossilized remains, experts have so far discovered more than 23 hominin species. Some are the direct ancestors of modern humans.

cut meat or crush bones.

Early learners

The oldest-known tools were shaped lumps of stone used for bashing and scraping. It took learning and skill to make tools with sharp cutting edges of the type used by *Homo habilis* – a clear sign of a more developed brain. *Homo habilis* means "skilled man".

Remains of animals killed by large predators were picked over by early humans.

Neanderthals

Neanderthals were a human-like species that lived in Europe for about 300,000 years before the first modern humans arrived. Neanderthals were similar to modern humans but shorter and stronger. Some had red hair and pale skin.

Neanderthal man

Built for the freezer

Neanderthals were able to survive several ice ages partly because their short arms and legs did not lose heat quickly. Their big, fleshy nose may have helped them to breathe more easily while hunting in freezing conditions.

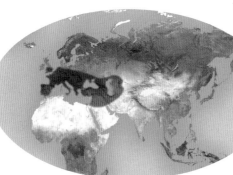

Map showing the locations (in brown) where Neanderthals lived

Where did they live?

Neanderthals lived all across Europe and into Turkey and Iran. Their name comes from the Neander Valley in Germany where their remains were first discovered in 1856.

Were they clever?

A Neanderthal's brain was actually bigger than that of a modern human. Neanderthals knew how to use fire and most scientists believe they had a basic language. They wore simple jewellery and, like us, buried their dead.

Neanderthals may have used body paint.

What did they eat?

Early people hunted large animals, such as bison and reindeer, at close range with spears and stone axes. They removed the fur and carved the meat using sharp stone scrapers or knives. Neanderthals also ate seals and cooked shellfish.

Bison

Wooden spear

Low, sloping forehead

High forehead

Neanderthal skull

Modern human skull

Head-to-head

Next to a modern human skull, a Neanderthal skull is longer and lower. Neanderthals also had large, round eye sockets with heavy brows, and large jaws with big front teeth.

Animal hides were perhaps used to make simple clothes.

Mussels

Modern humans

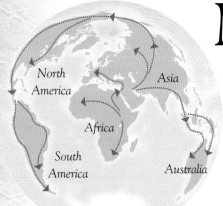

Map showing early human movement across the world

The first modern humans appeared in Africa 200,000 years ago. They looked exactly like people do today and were just as clever. Often living together in large groups, they learned how to make advanced tools and create amazing art.

Moving out

About 70,000 years ago, modern humans moved out of Africa. By 15,000 years ago, they had spread to every continent in the world, except for Antarctica. They travelled for trade or to follow migrating animal herds.

Barbed point made from bone

Tools they made

Early modern humans were highly skilled craftworkers. They made arrows and spears by attaching stone or bone points to wooden shafts. They also carved fine needles, harpoons, and fish hooks from bones and antlers.

Wise man

By 30,000 years ago, modern humans were probably the only human-like species remaining. They had a small, flat face, long, slender leg bones, fingers and thumbs skilled at gripping, and a large brain. This gave them the name *Homo sapiens*, or "wise man".

Early modern human working with stone tools

Group of tribesmen making traditional masks together

Necklace made from teeth and bones

What made them different?

Just like people today, early modern humans liked to look good. They probably used make-up and jewellery to show they belonged to a particular group.

NEANDERTHAL NEIGHBOURS

In Europe, modern humans and Neanderthals may have lived alongside each other for more than 40,000 years. Some modern humans and Neanderthals had children together, which means there is a tiny amount of Neanderthal in most modern Europeans.

Humans today

Although the human body hasn't changed much in 100,000 years, technology has transformed our planet and the way in which most of us behave. However, for a few isolated peoples, such as this group in Papua New Guinea, life has changed little for thousands of years.

The Stone Age

The Stone Age was a time in history when early humans used tools and weapons made out of stone. It lasted from when the first human-like species appeared about 3.4 million years ago until the introduction of metal tools a few thousand years ago.

Hand axe

A simple life

Homo habilis, or "handy man", lived in small groups. They gathered fruits and picked over animals killed by larger predators. They did not have strong teeth and used stone tools to break apart tough nuts, shells, and even bones to extract the marrow inside.

Sharp edge acted like the blade of a knife.

Scraper

Chopper

Grind, chop, and cut

The first tools were hand-held. Some, such as choppers, were used for crushing or grinding. Others had sharp edges to scrape away skin and fur, cut meat, or dig up roots. Hand axes appeared about 1.6 million years ago.

Hammerstone (stone used as a hammer to make tools)

Stone Age periods

● The Old Stone (Palaeolithic) Age lasted from the first use of stone tools until the end of the last Ice Age.

● The Middle Stone (Mesolithic) Age lasted from the end of the last Ice Age until the start of farming.

● The New Stone (Neolithic) Age lasted from the start of farming until the first use of metal.

How to knap

Early humans made tools out of stones, such as flint, by chipping away small flakes with a hammerstone. This is known as knapping.

First, strike hard with a hammerstone to chip away large flakes of stone.

Next, push down hard or grind the stone to create the right shape.

To finish, use bones and antlers to create a thin, sharp edge.

Did people live in caves?

Early humans lived in caves, but probably didn't stay in one place for long. Around 2 million years ago, the first-known man-made shelters appeared in eastern Africa. They were built from branches, leaves, mud, and piles of stones.

Did they wear clothes?

By studying head lice – tiny animals that sometimes live in our hair – experts believe that early humans began to wear clothes about 170,000 years ago.

A magnified view of lice

Flint blade

Who were the first farmers?

About 10,000 years ago, early humans in the Middle East learned how to grow cereals, such as wheat and barley, and how to store any surplus. Farming made it possible for people to settle down in one place.

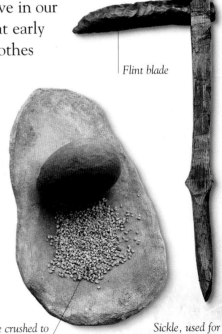

Cereals were crushed to make flour and pastes.

Grindstone

Sickle, used for harvesting crops

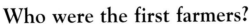

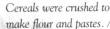

Living off the land

Early humans lived a "hunter-gatherer" lifestyle. Instead of growing their food, they went out and found it. They hunted and fished, gathered edible plants, took eggs from birds' nests, and, for a sweet treat, took honey from wild beehives.

Hazelnuts

Blackberries

Sharp end would be hardened in fire.

What's for tea?

Hunter-gatherers changed their diet with the seasons. In the summer and autumn there was a rich harvest of nuts, fruits, and berries. In winter, they relied more on meat.

Wooden spear

Let's fish!

Early people living near the sea used barbed spears to catch fish and, later, traps to catch eels, crabs, and lobsters.

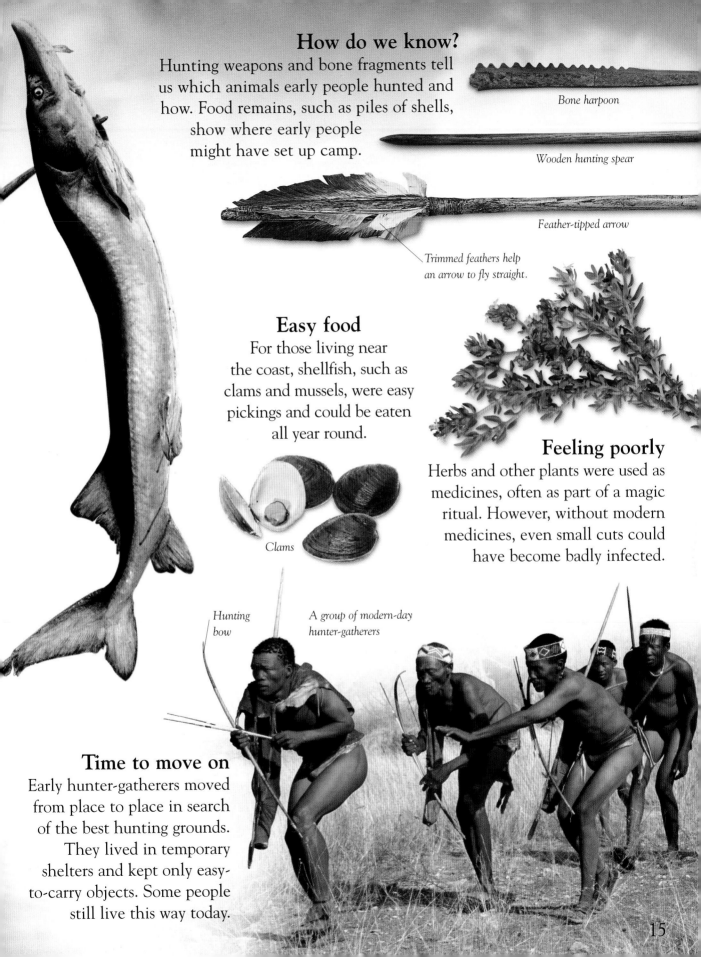

How do we know?

Hunting weapons and bone fragments tell us which animals early people hunted and how. Food remains, such as piles of shells, show where early people might have set up camp.

Bone harpoon

Wooden hunting spear

Feather-tipped arrow

Trimmed feathers help an arrow to fly straight.

Easy food

For those living near the coast, shellfish, such as clams and mussels, were easy pickings and could be eaten all year round.

Clams

Feeling poorly

Herbs and other plants were used as medicines, often as part of a magic ritual. However, without modern medicines, even small cuts could have become badly infected.

Hunting bow

A group of modern-day hunter-gatherers

Time to move on

Early hunter-gatherers moved from place to place in search of the best hunting grounds. They lived in temporary shelters and kept only easy-to-carry objects. Some people still live this way today.

15

The use of fire

Humans learned how to control fire more than a million years ago. Fire was used to light the way, keep away animals, and provide warmth. With fire, humans could camp and make a meal anywhere they chose, instead of having to seek out trees or rocks for shelter.

The heart of a home

About 250,000 years ago, early people started using a ring of stones, called a hearth, to contain a fire and protect it from the wind. In colder climates, the hearth was placed inside shelters for extra warmth.

How did they make fire?

Early humans first discovered fire made by lightning or bushfires. Later, they learned to create it. They spun a stick against wood until the heat set fire to dry grass. Then, they fanned the flames and added logs.

The Maasai in Africa still use

Party time!

A warm fire allowed people to gather in large groups and feel safe. The fireside was a good place to swap stories or talk to other people. Fires were probably the centre of feasts and rituals during the Stone Age, just as they are for all sorts of celebrations today.

Straw costumes and ogre masks

The Namahage festival in northern Honshu, Japan

A tasty meal

Eating cooked food made humans healthier, as it carried less disease. It was also a lot quicker to chew and digest. The extra energy may be why human brains grew almost twice as big in 500,000 years.

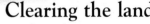

Spit held food over the flames

traditional methods to make fire.

Clearing the land

Stone Age humans found new ways to use fire. They used fire to clear land for farming, make pottery from clay, and around 5,000 years ago, create the first metal tools.

Life in the freezer

An ice age is a period of time, often thousands of years long, during which temperatures drop all over the world. Nearly 200,000 years ago, a few groups of humans survived an ice age by finding a small region with favourable living conditions on the coast of South Africa.

Fur-lined gloves

A land of snow

About 15,000 years ago, during the last Ice Age, glaciers and ice sheets up to 4 km (2 miles) thick covered the land. Life was tough, but Ice Age humans survived by living together, building shelters, and learning new hunting methods.

Spear

Why didn't they freeze?

To survive in the extreme cold, Ice Age humans lit fires to keep themselves warm. They sewed warm clothes from animal furs, as the Inuit peoples of the Arctic do today.

Modern-day needle and thread

What did they live in?

When other materials were hard to come by, early humans learned how to build houses using more unusual objects – including mammoth bones and tusks. The remains of one 44,000-year-old house contained more than 115 bones.

Follow the herd

Few fruits and plants could grow in the icy climate, so hunting was the main source of food. Ice Age humans followed herds of deer and mammoths through the cold and fog.

Bone houses would have been decorated with carvings and coloured paint.

Ice age facts

● Around 11 different ice ages have occurred during the last 4.6 billion years.

● The longest ice age lasted more than 100 million years.

● The ice sheets of Greenland and Antarctica and the world's glaciers are remnants from the last Ice Age.

Ross Ice Shelf in Antarctica

It's not over!

Believe it or not, we are still living in an ice age. Some places in the world, such as Antarctica, stay permanently frozen all year.

Land of the giants

Many large and dangerous animals flourished in the last Ice Age. Humans hunted some, such as mammoths, for food and tried to avoid others, such as sabre-toothed cats and giant cave bears.

Curved, sharp, 18-cm- (7-in-) long front teeth, or "sabres"

How do you hunt a mammoth?
Hunters probably targeted young, sick, or lone mammoths that had become trapped or stuck in a muddy swamp. After wounding their prey, the hunters waited until it collapsed, then moved in for the kill.

A nasty bite
Smilodon's long teeth look monstrous, but they could have broken easily. This sabre-toothed cat probably pounced on its prey from above, dug its "sabres" into the neck, and then backed off while the wounded animal bled to death.

A kangaroo for tea

The largest lizard in history, *Megalania* fed on giant kangaroos and giant wombats in prehistoric Australia. It not only had long, dagger-like teeth, but may also have poisoned its prey using deadly venom.

Megalania measured 5.5 m (18 ft) in length and weighed 600 kg (1,322 lb).

Megatherium means "great beast".

Mammoth tusks could grow up to 3 m (10 ft).

Megatherium measured up to 6 m (20 ft) in length.

Mega-sized claws

Megatherium was a giant ground sloth that lived in South America until about 10,000 years ago. This elephant-sized plant eater used its knife-like claws to grasp branches and rip the leaves off trees.

Frozen in time

In 2007, a near-perfectly preserved baby mammoth was found in northern Russia, 42,000 years after it had died. Its condition supports the idea that early humans may have stored their meat in ice-cold ponds, nature's own icebox.

The first artists

Early humans may have used art as a way of helping themselves in their struggle for survival. Paintings of animals are common. Perhaps this was thought to bring success when hunting or acted as a call for help from a spirit world they believed in.

Handprints were created on cave walls.

What did they use as paint?

Cave artists ground up coloured rock into a powder. This was mixed to a paste using spit, water, or animal fat, which helped the paint stick to the cave walls.

Yellow ochre

Red oxide powder

Charcoal (burnt wood) was also ground up to make paint.

A hand from the past

Over 40,000 years ago, cave dwellers created handprints by blowing paint through hollow bones. The prints were discovered in the El Castillo cave in northern Spain. This is the oldest-known cave art in Europe.

Paintings of bison, boars, and horses decorate the Lascaux cave in France.

How did they do it?
The famous cave paintings at Lascaux in southwest France are about 18,000 years old. The artists probably used their fingers, as well as twigs, moss, and horsehair brushes, to dab on the paint.

What's the oldest art?
About 75,000 years ago, artists in South Africa scratched patterns onto pieces of red rock. Later, Stone Age artists created sculptures and jewellery from clay, ivory, bone, or carved stone.

Bone engraved with the image of a bison

Mystery figures
Little statues of men, women, children, and animals have been found across Europe and Asia. Were they toys, statues of gods and goddesses, or self-portraits? Nobody knows!

A 25,000-year-old Venus figurine

ROCK ON!
Stone Age humans may have enjoyed making music as well as art. In 2008, a 35,000-year-old flute was found in Hohle Fels cave in Germany. It is made from a vulture's wing bone and has five fingerholes.

The first superhero?
Made out of mammoth bone, this "lion man" sculpture is about 40,000 years old. More than 30 cm (12 in) tall, it would have taken up to 400 hours to carve using tools made from stone.

23

Looking good

Just like people today, early humans used jewellery, clothing, tattoos, and make-up to change how they looked. Why? No one knows for sure. Having a tattoo or an earring may have shown they belonged to a particular group, or perhaps they just wanted to look good.

A Māori chief's tattooed mummified head

Get inked

Tattooing goes back a long way: in Jordan, a 10,000-year-old statue of a woman shows patterns pricked into her skin. Māori warriors in New Zealand were once heavily tattooed on their faces.

You missed a bit

Natural pigments have been used as body paint for thousands of years. Traces of red dye found beside the 75,000-year-old remains of a Neanderthal man have led experts to believe that the practice of body painting stretches far back into prehistory.

In Ethiopia, the Karo peoples are known for their body painting.

Fashion firsts

● Experts found shells strung together as beads in Blombos Cave, South Africa. These are the earliest-known man-made jewellery, created about 75,000 years ago.

● 9,000-year-old rock paintings in northern Africa show a woman with rows of dots running down her legs, arms, and body – the first signs of decorative body scars.

● About 6,000 years ago, women in western Asia used pastes made from crushed insects, red clay, or seaweed to colour their lips red.

Up to their necks

About 4,000 years ago, people in northern Europe wore metal neck rings to show wealth and power. Today, some cultures use neck rings for other reasons. Kayan women in Myanmar, for example, wear them to make their necks longer – a sign of beauty in their culture.

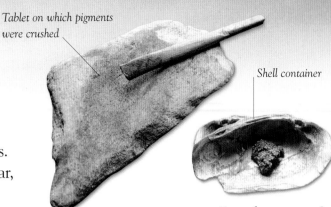

Tablet on which pigments were crushed

Shell container

Look at me!

Experts discovered what they believe to be 6,000-year-old make-up tools (above) in Turkey. Early people may have crushed pigments on stone surfaces and stored dyes in seashells.

Feather headdress

Wooden spatula is used to create patterns.

All ears

The earliest-known example of ear piercing has been found on a 5,000-year-old Egyptian mummy. The large plugs in his ears are similar to those worn by some South American peoples today.

25

The first religions

Early humans developed religious beliefs to help explain the world around them. They made up stories about why the Sun rose in the morning or why there were thunderstorms, and started worshipping such forces of nature. To keep their gods happy, they offered gifts and performed ceremonies.

Rest in peace

Neanderthals were the first humans to bury their dead: a sign that they may have believed in life after death. Rings of animal horns and flowers have been found in graves, along with useful things for the afterlife, such as stone tools.

Some bodies were tied up.

Were there priests?

Shamans and priests were important members of a tribe. They were thought to create a bridge to the spirit world, probably by dancing, singing, chanting, or going into a trance. They wore special costumes and headdresses.

Mayan priest performing a fire ceremony

House of the dead

To Stone Age peoples, a dark cave, a deep lake, or a snowy mountain top were all sacred places. Tombs, made of megaliths, were a link between the living and dead. Megalith comes from two Greek words: *mega*, meaning "big" and *lithos*, meaning "rock".

Charm made of leather, wood, bone, nuts, and cloth

Works like a charm

Without science to explain the world around them, early people were even more superstitious than we are today. They believed that amulets and charms had magical properties that would give them control over events in their life.

Charm used by the Nte'va people of central Africa

Oldest mummies

The deliberate preservation of a body by mummification showed a belief in an afterlife. The first mummies were naturally preserved by hot, dry conditions. The oldest, from South America, are about 9,000 years old.

Chinchorro mummy found in South America

Living with animals

While wild horses and cattle were probably originally hunted for their meat, dogs became our first pets. Then, about 10,000 years ago, early humans learned how to keep and use animals, such as sheep. For the first time, they had fresh supplies of meat, milk, and leather.

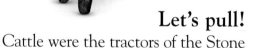

Cave painting in Algeria showing a hunter with a pet dog

Wild beginnings

The earliest dogs were actually wolves. More than 30,000 years ago, early humans started hunting with tamed wolves. One Israeli burial site contains the 12,000-year-old remains of a man hugging a puppy.

Let's pull!

Cattle were the tractors of the Stone Age, carrying and pulling far heavier loads than a person could. About 8,000 years ago, they dragged sledges and, later, hauled carts and ploughs.

Ships of the Andes

Llamas were first domesticated more than 6,000 years ago by people in the Andes mountains of South America. Llamas are still bred for their meat, wool, and manure, and used to carry heavy loads.

Peruvian llama herder

Eat up or giddy-up?

When ponies were first domesticated on the prairies of central Asia, they were kept for their meat, or used to pull carts or chariots. Only later, about 3,000 years ago, did anyone dare to jump up and ride them!

Sheep were the first animals to be bred for meat.

Were sheep always woolly?

Sheep once had hair like goats do today. People only kept them for meat and milk. Over hundreds of years, sheep were bred to have longer hair, which humans spun into wool.

29

Taming the land

Around 12,000 years ago, hunter-gatherers made an incredible discovery. They dug up the earth, scattered a few wild grains, and, as if by magic, food grew out of the ground. Humans had learned how to farm!

Let's farm there!
The first farmers lived in the Fertile Crescent. This region had a large number of plants and animals that could be used for farming.

Some of the first farms were in hilly areas, which had high rainfall.

Pop it in the pot
Early farmers no longer had to move about to find food. They began to live in permanent homes, raised animals, and invented heavy pots to store their surplus food in.

Who needs a tractor?

Farmers harvested their crops with stone tools, such as hoes for digging and axes for cutting. Some were made from obsidian – a glassy volcanic stone with sharp edges.

Adze with polished stone head

Mortar and pestle, used for grinding grain

Ancient model of a man using a plough

This is faster!

More than 8,000 years ago, farmers had a brainwave. They used cattle to pull a long pole with a spiked head to dig grooves into the soil for planting seeds: the first plough!

What's going on?

1. Small windows kept houses cool in summer. In winter, stoves kept them warm.

2. Cattle provided meat and leather, while sheep's wool was used to make clothes and rugs.

3. The first farmers grew crops such as wheat, barley, and peas.

4. They planted seeds in long rows or "furrows", dug using stone tools.

5. They learned to water the soil by digging ditches and canals.

6. They also may have lifted water from rivers using a device called a "shaduf".

The age of metal

The first metal objects were made by hammering chunks of soft metal, such as pure copper and gold, into shape. Later, people began to produce other metals by heating certain rocks. Some 6,000 years ago, they found a way to create an even harder metal – bronze.

Tin ore

Copper ore

The first miners

People gradually worked out that some rocks, known as ores, naturally contain metals. They dug pits or mines, set fires to crack open the rock, then broke it into smaller pieces with stone hammers.

Molten bronze

Mould

How was bronze made?

Bronze workers heated copper and tin together in a furnace. As the two metals melted, they combined to form liquid bronze. This was poured into clay or sand moulds (a method still in use).

One lump or two?

More than 4,000 years ago, Mediterranean merchants were trading pieces of copper and tin, known as ingots. About 2,700 years ago, discs of metal were used to make coins in China, India, and Greece.

Chinese copper coins

Bronze figurine

Works of art

Bronze was used to create tough, long-lasting weapons and tools. Craftworkers also learned how to create beautiful bronze ornaments and jewellery, often decorated with precious stones.

Iron shears for clipping wool

The Iron Age

Iron was one of the last metals to be used, as it needs a very hot fire to melt it. But iron is also easily found, so it quickly became the main material for early weapons and tools.

Bracelet

Skeleton buried with jewellery in Varna, Bulgaria

Gold disc

Buried treasure

Soft, easily shaped, and shiny, gold was used by early kings to show wealth and power. More than 900 gold ornaments were found in one 6,500-year-old grave in Varna, Bulgaria!

Weapons of war

From the beginning, early humans fought over food, water, and shelter, at first with simple spears and clubs, and later with bows and arrows. In time, small raids led to larger battles.

Oldest weapons

Early humans were using wooden spears with stone points more than 400,000 years ago. About 10,000 years ago, several new weapons appeared, including slings, daggers (short swords), and maces (a type of club).

Cave painting showing a war scene

Quill-tipped arrow

Quiver, which could hold more than a dozen arrows

Stone-tipped arrow

Bow is about 60 m (2 ft) long

Shoot!

The first bows and arrows appeared about 65,000 years ago. They could hit a target around 100 m (330 ft) away, twice as far as a thrown spear. Slings could hurl a stone even further, and more accurately. A fist-sized stone could break bones or smash skulls.

Mass-produced weapons

About 6,000 years ago, metalworkers in western Asia first learned how to forge spears, daggers, swords, and axes from bronze. When iron weapons appeared 3,000 years later, they were stronger, cheaper, and easier to produce. Weapons could now be made for thousands of soldiers.

ANCIENT VICTIMS

Perhaps the oldest evidence of warfare is Cemetery 117, a 14,000-year-old burial site found close to Egypt's Nile River. Here, the remains of 59 skeletons, including men, women, and children, were found. Many still had arrow heads or spear points stuck into them.

Re-enactment of a battle at a festival in Thailand

The first battles

As the first towns and cities grew larger, so did their armies. More than 4,000 years ago, Sargon the Great created the world's first empire in western Asia, thanks to his unstoppable army of archers, donkey chariots, and foot soldiers armed with spears.

Some ancient soldiers fought from the backs of horses, camels, and even elephants.

Ancient China

The first modern humans arrived in China about 70,000 years ago. Some 9,000 years ago, they began to grow grains such as millet, cabbages, and, eventually, rice; they also kept animals. In time, the first villages began to appear in fertile river valleys.

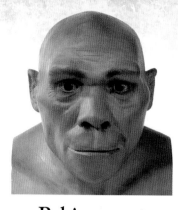

Peking mystery

Early humans lived in China a million years ago, hunting deer and cooking with fire. We know this from studies of the *Homo erectus* remains – known as "Peking Man" – which disappeared in 1941.

Farmers and hunters

As modern humans began to farm, some settled down along China's Yellow River. However, they continued to hunt: ancient village rubbish dumps are piled high with the bones of deer, wild cattle, antelopes, and hares.

Decorative grooves on the handle

Early pottery

Farmers stored their grain in large pots painted in red and black patterns. Skilled craftsmen moulded the complex shapes by hand. About 4,500 years ago, they started making delicate pottery using a potter's wheel.

Hand-moulded pottery

War and peace

Stone Age farmers in China lived in timber-and-mud houses with a sunken floor and steeply sloping thatched roof. Strong earth walls and weapons show that villagers also had to fend off attacks.

Smoke from the fire pit escaped through a hole in the roof.

Buried in time

In 1953, archaeologists discovered Banpo, a 6,500-year-old Stone Age farming village with 46 houses and more than 300 graves. Today, tourists can visit a reconstruction of the village.

Wooden support posts held up the roof.

Bone flutes

In 1999, six 9,000-year-old flutes were found in the Yellow River valley. They were made from the wing bones of birds called cranes. Incredibly, they could still be played!

Early Australia

Around 50,000 years ago, migrating humans reached a new continent – Australia. These hunter-gatherers roamed from place to place. They hunted animals using spears and boomerangs and gathered "bush tucker", such as wild fruits and seeds, shellfish, and emu eggs.

Carvings may help a boomerang to fly faster (just like the dimples on a golf ball).

Mungo Man

In 1974, the remains of Australia's earliest-known person were found in a 40,000-year-old burial site in Lake Mungo, in the southeastern part of Australia.

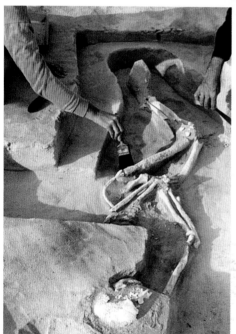

The first people had 300 different languages.

First peoples

The first humans to reach Australia were the ancestors of modern-day peoples. European settlers later called them Aborigines, meaning "first peoples". They form one of the world's oldest continuous cultural traditions. Seen here are modern Aboriginal people participating in a traditional dance festival.

Throwing sticks

The earliest boomerang found in Australia is 10,000 years old. A skilled hunter can throw this curved weapon more than 200 m (656 ft). It can also be used as a knife, hammer, digging tool, or even for tapping out a rhythm!

Turf or surf?

Early Australian peoples were skilled trackers. They hunted animals such as snakes, kangaroos, bats, and emus. Peoples living near the coast ate a lot of shellfish, and used spears to hunt fish, turtles, stingrays, and whales.

Red kangaroo

Ahoy there!

Early sailors must have been incredibly brave. It's thought some crossed rough seas on simple rafts or in canoes to reach Sahul, an ancient continent that combined modern-day Australia (including Tasmania) and New Guinea.

Benches for paddlers

Outrigger keeps the canoe stable in rough seas.

Thin hull, or body, built for speed

Pacific Islanders

Thousands of islands – called the Pacific Islands – to the north and east of Australia were first settled around 2000 BCE. One group of people, known as the Lapita, were skilled sailors. They invented the outrigger canoe that allowed them to travel far and wide.

39

The Americas

Modern humans crossed over from northern parts of Asia to America about 15,000 years ago. Gathering fruits, nuts, and roots along the way, they spread across the continent, tracking herds of deer, mammoths, camels, and antelopes.

Squashes

Super sharp tools

Early Americans learned how to craft sharp spearheads by chipping fine flakes from stone. They also invented the atlatl – a spear-thrower that allowed them to hunt from a distance.

Over the edge

The first Americans learned how to make animals stampede into watery bogs or over cliffs. At Head-Smashed-In Buffalo Jump in Alberta, Canada, huge numbers of buffalo skeletons still lie next to stone arrowheads and pits where hunters boiled the bones.

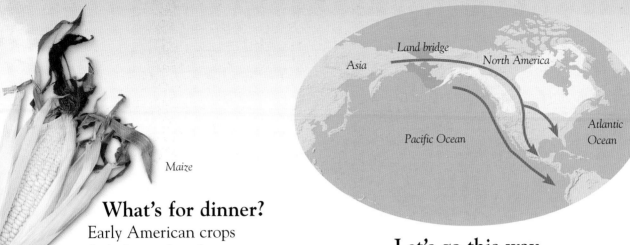
Maize

What's for dinner?
Early American crops included squashes, beans, potatoes, and, later, maize. Animals such as fish, birds, and buffalo were hunted for meat, while llamas and guinea pigs were bred for food in parts of South America.

Let's go this way
Most experts agree that the first modern humans arrived in North America from Asia by walking across what is now the Bering Strait. In the last Ice Age, this was a land bridge. From Alaska, they spread to the rest of the continent. It is also thought that people arrived in America along the coast.

An exciting discovery
The remains of a dozen huts found at Monte Verde in Chile, in 1976, provided proof that modern humans were living in South America at least 14,000 years ago. They harvested seaweed (still farmed in the area today) and were the first people known to have eaten potatoes.

The big goodbye
By 10,000 years ago, most large mammals in the Americas had become extinct, including giant beavers the size of bears. Experts believe that the arrival of human hunters may have caused these animals to die out.

Giant beavers, which grew up to 2.5 m (8 ft) long

41

The first towns

Once people could grow more food than they needed, they began trading with their neighbours. About 7,500 years ago, as many as 6,000 people, including farmers, weavers, and potters, were living together in Çatalhöyük, a bustling town in what is now Turkey.

The walls had no windows or doors.

Walls were made of mud bricks coated with plaster, which was replaced every year.

Shelter made of woven cloth

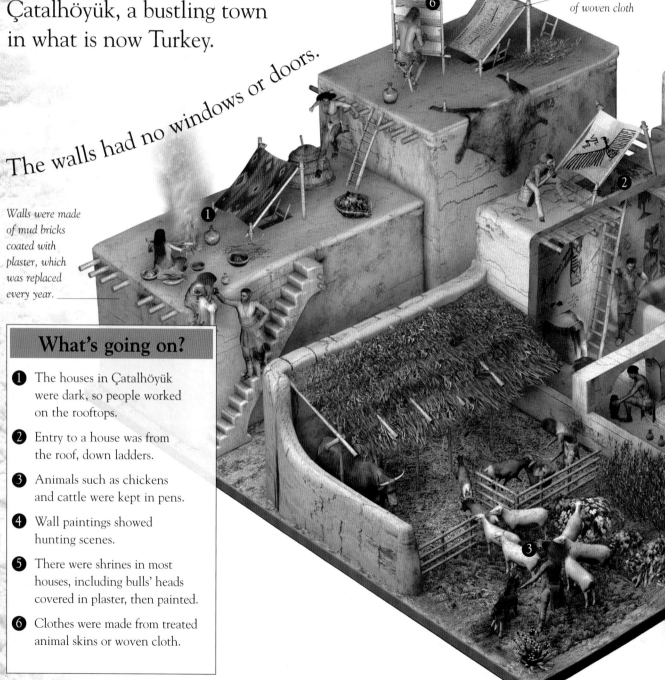

What's going on?

1. The houses in Çatalhöyük were dark, so people worked on the rooftops.

2. Entry to a house was from the roof, down ladders.

3. Animals such as chickens and cattle were kept in pens.

4. Wall paintings showed hunting scenes.

5. There were shrines in most houses, including bulls' heads covered in plaster, then painted.

6. Clothes were made from treated animal skins or woven cloth.

Donkeys, kings, and kilts

Mosaics from the Sumerian city of Ur, now in Iraq, show scenes of city life more than 4,500 years ago. Here, men and donkeys form a procession. Another scene shows a king wearing a kilt!

Long live the king!

The world's earliest-known kings ruled in ancient Sumer. Each of Sumer's 30 cities also had a ruler. So far, 27 statues have been found of one ruler, Gudea.

Statue of Sumerian ruler Gudea

Early writing

The Sumerians kept records by making wedge-shaped marks (called cuneiform) on clay tablets. In China, messages to the gods were carved onto pieces of bone and turtle shell.

Sumerian cuneiform tablet

Çatalhöyük people buried their dead under the floor of their homes so that they were never far away.

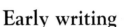

What's missing?

One thing that wasn't used in Çatalhöyük was the wheel – because it hadn't been invented. The wheel first appeared some 5,500 years ago, and has been used continuously since then.

How do we know?

Archaeologists study the remains of ancient people and objects. By investigating the remains of a 5,300-year-old frozen mummy, nicknamed "Ötzi the Iceman", experts found clues about how early humans lived as well as uncovering an ancient murder mystery.

Bread

Sloes

Who found the body?

In 1991, a pair of German hikers stumbled across a well-preserved body in the Ötztal Alps, Italy. Half the body was still frozen in ice, and had to be cut out using drills and ice-axes.
This was Ötzi.

Last supper

Bread, sloes (berries), and deer meat were found in Ötzi's stomach. The fact his body didn't have time to digest his last meal suggests that he might have been caught in a surprise attack!

Ice around the body was found to contain objects that had belonged to Ötzi.

Only the top half of the body was visible.

Clues to the past

Animal hairs found on Ötzi's clothing showed that he herded sheep and goats. He carried wooden tools for making clothing, a copper axe, and a bow and arrow (which he had leaned against a nearby tree before he died).

DNA tests tell us that Ötzi had brown eyes.

Life-size model of Ötzi on display at a museum in Austria

That's him!

In 2011, scientists used computer graphics and scans of Ötzi's skull to rebuild his face. They found he had deep-set brown eyes and a long, hooked nose.

Wooden spear

Knife sheath

Meet Ötzi!

The ice preserved Ötzi's body amazingly well. We know he was about 1.6 m (5.3 ft) tall and weighed 50 kg (110 lb). We even know he had weak knees! He wore leather shoes and goatskin leggings, and had tattoos on his body.

HOW DID HE DIE?

At first, it seemed as if Ötzi had died following a bash on the head. But after studying scans of his body, archaeologists think Ötzi probably bled to death after being wounded in the shoulder by an arrow.

Leggings and boots tied together

True or false?

It's time to test your knowledge about early people. See if you can spot what is true and what is false in this mini quiz.

Early humans first **rode horses** and then used them to carry loads.
See page 29

Neanderthals lived in **South America**.
See page 8

Farmers used stone **mortar and pestles** to grind grains.
See page 31

There are **27 known statues** of the Sumerian king Gudea.
See page 43

Early people first **created fire** using lightning or bushfires.
See page 16

People living in Çatalhöyük used **the wheel**.
See page 43

Ötzi had bread, sloes, and deer meat for his last meal.
See page 44

The earliest **swords and daggers** were made of iron.
See page 35

Early Chinese **pottery** was moulded by hand.
See page 36

The **first plough** was invented more than 8,000 years ago.
See page 31

Megalania, a plant eater, used its giant claws to rip off leaves.
See page 21

Head for home

Life in prehistoric times wasn't easy. Help this Neanderthal find his way home, but watch out for dangers along the way!

FINISH
You reached your settlement!

Ride a horse.
Go ahead 3

Attacked by a group of hunters.
Move back 3

Discover how to create fire.
Go ahead 4

How to play

This game is for up to four players.

You will need
- A dice
- Counters – one for each player.

Move down   **Move up**

Trace over the wheel outlines below, or cut and colour your own from card. Each player takes turns to throw the dice, and begins from the START box. Follow the squares with each roll of the dice. If you land on an instruction, make sure you do as it says. Good luck!

Path blocked by a *Smilodon*.
Move back 5

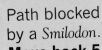

Use leaves to collect water. **Go ahead 2**

Held up by a hailstorm. **Move back 5**

Find berries to eat on the way. **Go ahead 2**

Stop at a cave to paint. **Miss a turn**

Stop to hunt for fish. **Miss a turn**

Find a lucky charm. **Go ahead 3**

Hit by a boomerang. **Move back 2**

START

49

What's this?

Take a look at these close-ups of pictures in the book, and see if you can identify them. The clues should help you.

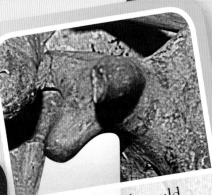

- These animals could carry heavy loads.
- 8,000 years ago, people used them to pull sledges.

See page 28

- These paintings are 18,000 years old.
- They were probably made using fingers, twigs, and moss.

See page 23

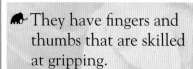

- They have fingers and thumbs that are skilled at gripping.
- Their name translates as "wise man".

See page 10

- Ancient Sumerians kept records on this.
- Wedge-shaped marks were made on its surface.

See page 43

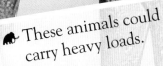

- People found a way to make this metal some 6,000 years ago.
- Bronze and tin are melted to make this.

See page 32

 This animal would bite its prey and then wait until it bled to death.

 Its long front teeth are also called "sabres".

See page 20

 This person lived 5,300 years ago.

 We know what he looked like.

See page 45

 This was used by the Nte'va people in Africa.

 It was thought to have magical properties.

See page 27

 This metal is shiny, soft, and easily shaped.

 It was used by kings to show wealth and power.

See page 33

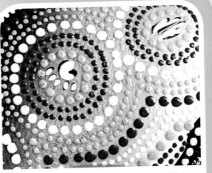

 Hunters used it as a knife, hammer, or digging tool.

 The earliest example of this in Australia is 10,000 years old.

See page 39

 These are tiny animals that live on our bodies.

 They help experts learn about clothes early humans wore.

See page 13

Which way?

This little boy is caught in a storm. Answer each question correctly to help him reach the safe shelter of the cave.

hunting animals

During an ice age, the main source of food came from...
See page 19

gathering fruits

growing crops

"Middle Stone"

"first peoples"

"handy person"

"Mesolithic" means...
See page 12

copper and tin

gold and tin

Bronze was created by mixing...
See page 32

iron and gold

START

the first Americans

Shamans are...
See page 26

FINISH

Sumerian kings

preserved in ice

spiritual guides

alive and healthy

Ötzi was found...
See page 44

a type of cat with long front teeth

sick and dying

A Smilodon was...
See page 20

an elephant-like animal

a type of reindeer

Glossary

Here are the meanings of some words that are
useful to know when learning about early people.

Adze a stone tool similar to an axe, often used for shaping wood.

Archaeologist a scientist who studies the past, by looking at ancient remains such as bones and tools.

Atlatl a spear-throwing tool used by hunters in Australia and North America.

Banpo an 8,000-year-old village discovered in 1953 in the Yellow River valley, China.

Boomerang a curved throwing stick used by Stone Age hunters. When thrown the right way, it returns to the hunter.

Bronze Age a period when people first learned to mix copper and tin to make bronze.

Climate average weather in a region over many years. While the weather can change in an instant, the climate can take thousands or even millions of years to change.

Cuneiform wedge-shaped marks made on clay tablets, used by the ancient Sumerians.

Early humans early members of the group *Homo*, dating back some 2.4 million years to the emergence of *Homo habilis*.

Empire a group of nations or peoples with one powerful ruler.

Extinction a process by which one or more groups of a plant or animal die out completely.

Fertile Crescent crescent-shaped region stretching from the Mediterranean Sea to the Persian Gulf. Many of the earliest towns and settlements appeared here.

Fossil remains of an ancient plant or animal, preserved in rock.

Furnace an enclosed structure in which heat is produced, often for melting metals.

Furrow a long, narrow trench in the ground made by a plough, for planting seeds.

Glacier a slow-moving mass of ice.

Hand axe an oval or pear-shaped stone with a sharp edge, used by early humans for cutting plants and scraping meat.

Hominin a scientific term for humans and our ancestors.

Homo sapiens the only surviving human species. The words comes from two Latin words, which mean "wise man".

Hunter-gatherers early humans who hunted wild animals and collected wild plants for food.

Ice age a period in the Earth's history when the whole planet was much colder. The most recent ice age lasted from around 35,000 to 12,000 years ago, when large sheets of ice covered most of northern Europe and North America.

Knapping chipping away at a stone with sharp blows to create a tool or weapon.

Land bridge a stretch of land in prehistoric times, now covered by sea, that once joined two continents or a large island to a continent.

Megalith a large rock, often weighing several tonnes, used to build a prehistoric monument.

Migration movement of a large group of people or animals from one place to another.

Mummy body of a human or animal, preserved by hot sand, ice, or chemicals.

Prairie a large area of grassland, such as in North America.

Prehistoric anything more than 3,000 years old, before written records began.

Shaduf a simple device for lifting water; used by early farmers to water their crops.

Shaman a religious leader in a group or tribe that people believe can talk to the spirit world and cure the sick.

Species a group of living things that can breed with each other to give birth to young.

Stone Age a period when metal was unknown: tools were made of stone, wood, bone, or antlers.

Tattoo a type of body art where a permanent design is made on skin with a needle and ink.

A still from the film
The Clan of the Cave Bear

Index

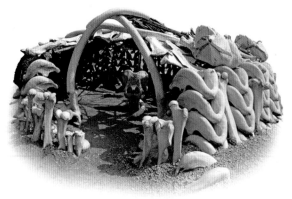

Aboriginal people 38-39
Africa 4, 10, 13, 18, 27
America 40-41
ancestors 7
animals 20-21
arrow 15, 34
artists 22-23
Australia 38-39
Australopithecus 4-5

Banpo 37
body painting 24-25
boomerang 39
bow 13, 34
brain 6, 8, 10, 17
bronze 32-33

canoe 39
Çatalhöyük 42-43
caves 13, 28
  cave paintings 22-23, 34
China 36-37, 43
clothing 13
coins 32-33
crops 31, 41

ear piercing 25

farming 13, 17, 30-31
Fertile Crescent 30
fire 16-17
food 9, 14, 15, 17, 39,
  41, 44

giant beaver 41
Gudea 43

hammerstone 12
handprints 22
herbs 13
hominin 4, 7
Homo erectus 7, 36
Homo ergaster 7
Homo habilis 6, 7
Homo heidelbergensis 7
houses 13, 19, 37, 42-43
hunter-gatherers 14-15,
  30, 38
hunting 9, 20-21, 40, 46

ice age 8, 12, 18-19, 20, 41
iron 32-33, 35

jewellery 11, 24, 33

Karo, Ethiopia 24-25
knapping 13

land bridge 41
language 8, 9, 38
Lapita 39
lice 13
"Lucy" 5

make-up 11, 25
mammoths 19, 20-21,
  23, 40
medicine 15
Megalania 21
megalith 27
Megatherium 21
Mesolithic 12
metal 32-33
modern humans 7, 10-11,
  36, 40, 41
  skull 9
Monte Verde 41
mummies 24, 25, 27, 44

Mungo Man 38
music 23, 37

Neanderthals 7, 8-9, 26
Neolithic 12
Nutcracker Man 5

Ötzi 44-45

Pacific Islands 39
Palaeolithic 12
plough 28, 31

religion 26-27

sabre-toothed cat,
  see *Smilodon*
sailors 39
shaman 26
skeleton 5
skulls 9
Smilodon 20
Stone Age 12-13, 17, 23,
  27, 28, 37

tattoos 24
tombs 27
tools 7, 12, 13, 17, 31, 40
towns 42-43

Venus figurine 23

weapons 34-35
wheel 43
writing 43

Acknowledgements

Dorling Kindersley would like to thank Andy Cooke for artwork and Annabel Blackledge for proofreading.

Picture credits

The publisher would like to thank the following for their kind permission to reproduce their photographs:
(Key: a-above; b-below/bottom; c-centre; f-far; l-left; r-right; t-top)
2-3 **Corbis:** Marc Dozier. 3 **Alamy Images:** Arterra Picture Library (br). 4 **Science Photo Library:** John Reader (l, bc). 5 **Alamy Images:** Sabena Jane Blackbird (tl). **Corbis:** Christophe Boisvieux (tr). **Science Photo Library:** P.Plailly / E.Daynes (br). 6 **Getty Images:** Photolibrary / Martin Harvey (cla). 6-7 **Dorling Kindersley:** Rough Guides (b). 7 **Alamy Images:** Cro Magnon (tr); Visual&Written SL (tc/Homo Ergaster); PhotoStock-Israel (cr). **Corbis:** Science Picture Co.- (tl, tc/ Homo Habilis). 9 **123RF.com:** Eric Isselee (tr). **Alamy Images:** E.R. Degginger (cr). 10 **Alamy Images:** Arterra Picture Library (bl). **Science Photo Library:** Natural History Museum, London (c). 11 **Corbis:** Marc Dozier (b). **SuperStock:** DeAgostini / DeAgostini (tl). 12 **Dorling Kindersley:** The Natural History Museum, London (cra/Scraper, cra/Flint Handaxe). 13 **Alamy Images:** Paul Olding (cla). **Dorling Kindersley:** The Museum of London (br/Stone Quern). **Photoshot:** Bandphoto / Uppa.co.uk (bl). 14 **Dorling Kindersley:** The Museum of London (tl). **Science Photo Library:** P.Plailly / E.Daynes (b). 15 **Alamy Images:** John Warburton-Lee Photography (br). **Dorling Kindersley:** The Museum of London (tr/Harpoon, tr/Spear). **Dreamstime.com:** Shariff Che\' Lah (c). 16 **Dreamstime.com:** Alexandr Vasilyev (cla). 16-17 **123RF.com:** David Tyrer (b). **Dreamstime.com:** Fotoplanner. 17 **Alamy Images:** JTB MEDIA CREATION, Inc. (tl). **Getty Images:** Altrendo Images (cr); Gamma-Rapho via Getty Images (br). 18 **Science Photo Library:** Henning Dalhoff. 19 **Dreamstime.com:** Yulia Gapeenko (tl). **Getty Images:** Oxford Scientific / Rick Price (br); Photographer's Choice RF / Luis Davilla (tr). **Glowimages:** SuperStock (br). 22-23 **Science Photo Library:** CM Dixon (clb). 22 **Science Photo Library:** Tom Mchugh (bl). 23 **Dorling Kindersley:** The University Museum of Archaeology and Anthropology, Cambridge (cl); The Natural History Museum, London (cr). **Glowimages:** SuperStock (br). 24-25 **Alamy Images:** Ariadne Van Zandbergen (b). 24 **Corbis:** DPA / Tobias Kleinschmidt (tr). 25 **Alamy Images:** Danita Delimont (crb); Nathan Benn (r). **Rex Features:** KeystoneUSA-ZUMA (tl). 26 **Science Photo Library:** Tom Mchugh (bl). 26-27 **Alamy Images:** Yvette Cardozo (r). 27 **Dorling Kindersley:** Pitt Rivers Museum, University of Oxford (cr). **Getty Images:** UIG via Getty Images (br). 28-29 **Alamy Images:** William Arthur (b). 28 **Alamy Images:** DPK-Photo (cl); World Religions Photo Library; Elitsa Lambova (tl). 29 **Corbis:** Hemis / Morandi Bruno (tl); Michael S. Yamashita (cr). 30 **Corbis:** Gianni Dagli Orti (tr). 30-31 **Steve Haasis (www.ancientvine.com).** 31 **Alamy Images:** The Art Archive (tr). **Dorling Kindersley:** The Science Museum, London (tl). **Getty Images:** Hulton Archive / Print Collector (cla). 32 **Corbis:** Science Faction / Mark Alberhasky (l). **Dorling Kindersley:** The Natural History Museum, London (cr). 33 **Alamy Images:** Edwin Baker (b). **Dreamstime.com:** Donkeyru (tr). **Getty Images:** DEA / G. Dagli Orti (tl); The Bridgeman Art Library (c). 34 **Corbis:** Pierre Colombel (cla). **Dorling Kindersley:** Pitt Rivers Museum, University of Oxford (clb). 34-35 **Alamy Images:** Dave Stamboulis (b). 35 **Science Photo Library:** Ria Novosti (tl). 36 **Alamy Images:** DBimages (cl); The Natural History Museum (tr); The Art Archive (bl). 36-37 **Getty Images:** De Agostini Picture Library. 37 **Brookhaven National Laboratory:** (br). **Ian Armstrong-https://www.flickr.com/photos/97725124@N00/:** (tr). 38 **Press Association Images:** AP / University of Melbourne, HO (clb). 38-39 **Alamy Images:** Ozimages. 39 **Alamy Images:** Douglas Peebles Photography (crb). **Dorling Kindersley:** Rough Guides (ca/Grass). **Dreamstime.com:** Ashwin Kharidehal Abhirama (tl). 40 **Dorling Kindersley:** The American Museum of Natural History (cla). **Getty Images:** Nativestock / Marilyn Angel Wynn (b). 40-41 **Dorling Kindersley:** Rough Guides. 41 **Getty Images:** AFP / Stringer / Ariel Marinkovic (crb). 42-43 **Alamy Images:** World History Archive (t). 42 **Dreamstime.com:** Keantian (b). 43 **123RF.com:** James Steidl (bc). **Alamy Images:** DEA / G. Dagli Orti (tr). 44 **123RF.com:** stargatechris (tr). **Getty Images:** Gamma-Rapho Via Getty Images / Paul Hanny (b). 45 **Alamy Images:** Martin Shields (r). **South Tyrol Museum Of Archaeology - www.iceman.it:** (tl, clb). 46 **Getty Images:** DEA / G. Dagli Orti (clb); Hulton Archive / Print Collector (cb). 47 **123RF.com:** James Steidl (tl). **Alamy Images:** The Art Archive. **Dorling Kindersley:** Andrew Kerr (b). **Getty Images:** DEA / G. Dagli Orti (cr). **Science Photo Library:** Ria Novosti (tl). 48 **Alamy Images:** PhotoStock-Israel (cb, crb). 49 **123RF.com:** stargatechris. **Alamy Images:** PhotoStock-Israel (c, ca). **Dorling Kindersley:** Pitt Rivers Museum, University of Oxford (clb). **Dreamstime.com:** stargatechris (cb). 50 **Alamy Images:** Arterra Picture Library (cl); World Religions Photo Library; Elitsa Lambova (bc). **Corbis:** Science Faction / Mark Alberhasky (b). **Dreamstime.com:** Ashwin Kharidehal Abhirama (tr). **Science Photo Library:** Pascal Goetgheluck (cr). 51 **Alamy Images:** Arterra Picture Library (bl); Edwin Baker (cl). **Dorling Kindersley:** Pitt Rivers Museum, University of Oxford (tr). **Dreamstime.com:** (c). **Photoshot:** Bandphoto / Uppa.co.uk (cr). **South Tyrol Museum Of Archaeology - www.iceman.it:** (tc). 52 **Getty Images:** DEA / G. Dagli Orti (bc). 53 **Alamy Images:** Martin Shields (c); Yvette Cardozo (tl). **Dorling Kindersley:** Jon Hughes and Russell Gooday (bc). 54-55 **Alamy Images:** AF archive. 56 **Glowimages:** CM Dixon. 58 **Dorling Kindersley:** Andrew Kerr (br); The Natural History Museum, London (tl, tr, fcla, ca, cb/Handaxe); The Science Museum, London (tc); National Museum of Wales (tc/Baby Mammoth); The American Museum of Natural History (cl); The University Museum of Archaeology and Anthropology, Cambridge (c, clb); Pitt Rivers Museum, University of Oxford (c/Pebble Hammer); The Museum of London (cr). 59 **Dorling Kindersley:** Andrew Kerr (br); The University Museum of Archaeology and Anthropology, Cambridge (cl); The Natural History Museum, London (cr). **Dreamstime.com:** Ashwin Kharidehal Abhirama (tr). **Science Photo Library:** Pascal Goetgheluck (cr); The Natural History Museum, London (tl, tr, fcla, ca, cb/Handaxe); Pitt Rivers Museum, University of Oxford (ftl, tr, cl, cr, clb, cb/Fire Drill); The Museum of London (fcl, cb, crb); The American Museum of Natural History (bl). 62 **Dorling Kindersley:** Jon Hughes and Russell Gooday (bl); The American Museum of Natural History (tl); The University Museum of Archaeology and Anthropology, Cambridge (tc, cla, cr); The Science Museum, London (tr); The Statens Historiska Museum, Stockholm (fcla); The Combined Military Services Museum (CMSM) (c); The National Museum of Wales (cb); The Natural History Museum, London (bc, br). 63 **Dorling Kindersley:** Jon Hughes (ftl); Rough Guides (tl); The University Museum of Archaeology and Anthropology, Cambridge (tc, fcl); The Oxford Museum of Natural History (cla); The American Museum of Natural History (ca, fbl); Simon Jackson Carter (cra); The Natural History Museum, London (cla/Handaxe, bc, bc/Venus); Pitt Rivers Museum, University of Oxford (fcla, cr, bl, b/Bow); The Museum of London (fcr)

All other images © Dorling Kindersley
For further information see: www.dkimages.com